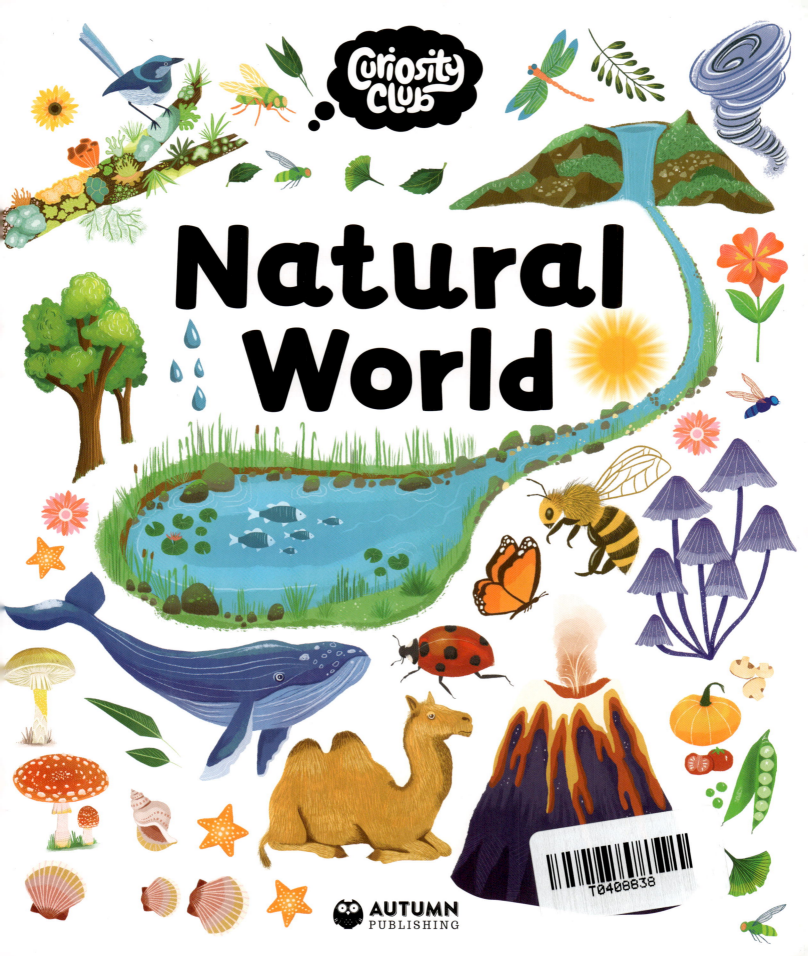

Look out for these key words:

Biome: a large ecosystem that relies on climate and terrain.

Carnivore: an animal that feeds on other animals.

Climate: the weather and temperature of a place.

Environment: the surroundings in which a living thing exists.

Habitat: where a plant or animal lives.

Herbivore: an animal that feeds on plants.

Invertebrate: an animal that does not have a backbone.

Omnivore: an animal that eats both plants and other animals.

Seasons: the four periods of a year—spring, summer, autumn, and winter.

Species: a group of living things with the same characteristics.

Tectonic Plates: large, solid sections of the Earth's crust.

Vertebrate: an animal that has a backbone.

Contents

What Being Alive Is..................6
Habitats and Biomes..................8
How Plants and Animals Are Grouped..................10
Food Chains..................12
Flowering Plants..................14
All About Trees..................16
Nature We Eat..................18
Mushrooms and Other Fungi..................20
Underground World..................22
Grasslands and Desert..................24
Arctic and Antarctic..................26
Tropical and Polar Oceans..................28
Lakes, Ponds, and Swamps..................30
Running Water..................32
Mountains and Caves..................34
Volcanoes..................36
Earthquakes and Tsunamis..................38
Hurricanes and Tornadoes..................40
Weather and Seasons..................42
Climate Change..................44
Index..................46

What Being Alive Is

Did you know that there are seven things an organism must do to be seen as "alive"?

Move

Animals (including humans like us!) can run, fly, swim, and slither. Plants or corals stay in one place but have moving parts. For example, sunflowers turn toward sunlight, and daisies open and close their petals.

Reproduce

Some animals give birth to live young, while others lay eggs. Plants spread spores or seeds to grow the next generation.

Some clever animals change their bodies to suit their environment. Frogs begin their lives as tadpoles, then become frogs who can live in and out of the water.

Adapt/Respond

All living things react to the world around them. Plants can send roots into the ground in search of water, and animals adapt to their surroundings— even changing color when they need to!

The male Vogelkop bird has adapted to be quite a show-off! He dances and parades his colorful feathers in order to attract a mate.

Absorb Energy

Animals absorb their energy through food, while some plants can make their own food by absorbing energy from the Sun.

Breathe

Nearly all living things need oxygen to survive—and they get this in lots of different ways. From breathing to absorbing sunlight. This is called "respiration."

Excrete

All living beings need to "get rid" of the things they take in but don't need. Animals breathe out carbon dioxide, while plants get rid of oxygen. Feces (poop) and urine (pee) are also forms of excretion.

Grow

All organisms grow and change over their lifetime. Mammals (like us) have a skeleton that grows with them. Plants develop from seeds or bulbs, while caterpillars change entirely when they transform into butterflies!

Habitats and Biomes

Earth is a perfect puzzle of different habitats and biomes. Each one has its own climate, wildlife, and flora (plant life), creating diverse homes for all life.

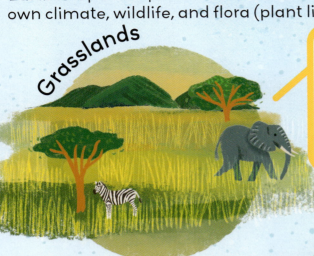

Grasslands

Grasslands are large areas of land where the main plant grown is grass. For that reason, it makes a great home for herbivores such as elephants, zebras, and antelope. Grasslands are found all over the world, but the largest grasslands are in Australia and North America.

Temperate Forests

Temperate forests are mild and rainy. Warmer areas include evergreen trees (that bloom all year round) like eucalyptus, that make the perfect homes for koalas. Cooler parts have deciduous trees (that drop their leaves) that are great for badgers and deer to live among.

Over 70 percent of Earth is covered by oceans. Warm, colorful coral reefs and dark, icy trenches all provide homes for a wide variety of life, from gigantic whales to tiny plankton.

Coniferous Forests

Wetlands are anywhere that land is covered by water, such as ponds, rivers, lakes, and marshes. The West Siberian Lowland is one of the largest wetlands in the world.

Oceans

Wetlands

Coniferous forests grow in places with long, cold winters where animals like wolves and bears like to hibernate. Trees here are cone-shaped and evergreen, providing food and shelter for lots of different animals.

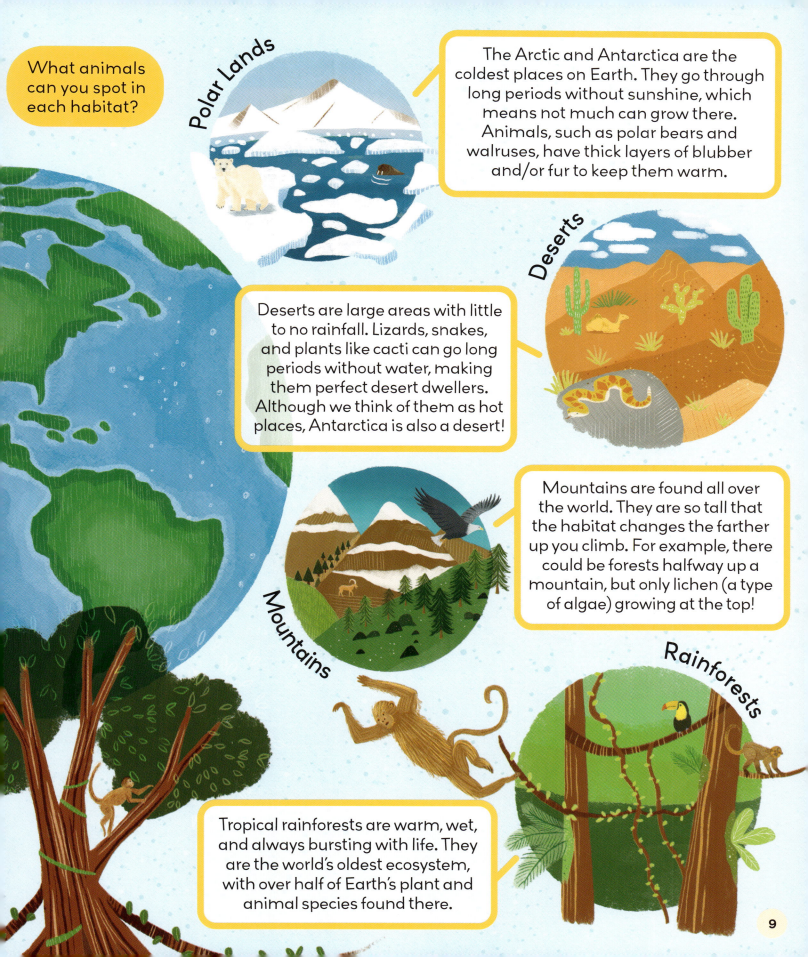

How Plants and Animals Are Grouped

All living things can feed, grow, reproduce, and release waste—but each one does it differently. Almost every organism can fit into one of these categories...

Plants

Plants can be split into flowering and non-flowering groups.

Non-flowering plants only grow leaves.

Flowering plants have petals and are often colorful.

Fungi

Fungi is the name given to mushrooms, molds, and yeasts.

Moss and Liverworts

Moss and liverworts are a collection of tiny plants that love damp, shady spots.

Vertebrates

Vertebrates have backbones.

Mammals give birth to live young. Marsupials, like this koala bear, are also mammals, but their young are carried in pouches after they are born until they are ready for the world.

Animals

Animals can be split into two main categories.

Invertebrates

Invertebrates do not have backbones. Instead, they have exoskeletons like a shell or hard skin (an "outside" skeleton).

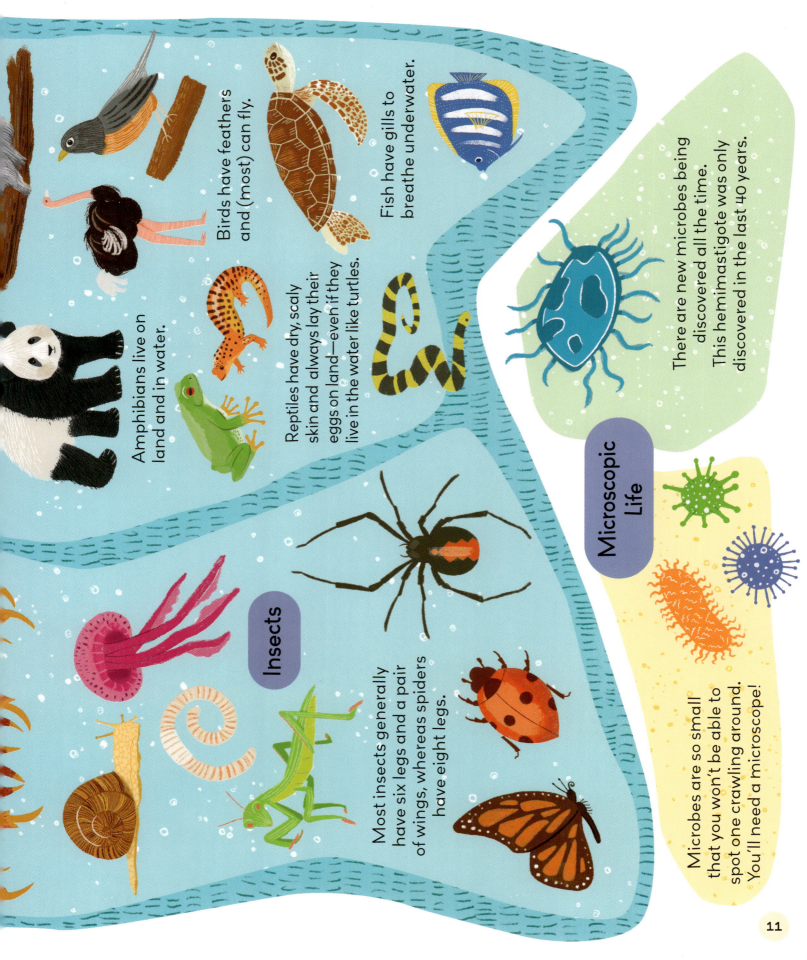

Food Chains

All living things eat. Some are meat eaters (carnivores), some are plant eaters (herbivores), and some eat both (omnivores). A zebra is a herbivore, as it eats red grass. A lion is a carnivore and eats zebras. This is called a food chain! Take a look at some other food chains below.

Decomposers and Producers	Primary Consumers	Secondary Consumers
These are usually plants, fungi or tiny microorganisms.	Small animals and herbivores.	Small creatures that are carnivores or omnivores.

Grass →	Grasshopper →	Rat
Plankton →	Krill →	Fish larvae
Pond algae →	Caddisfly →	Pond fish

12

Tertiary Consumers	Scavengers and Apex Predators
Animals that eat both primary and secondary consumers.	Scavengers feed off animals that are already dead. Apex predators are at the top of the food chain!

Snake

Hawk

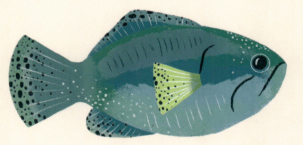

Tuna

Great White Shark

Kingfisher

DID YOU KNOW?

Not every habitat has an apex predator. In some places, the tertiary consumer—like this kingfisher—is the top of the food chain and doesn't need to worry about being hunted. This doesn't mean that it is safe if it leaves its usual environment, though!

13

All About Trees

Trees are pretty amazing. They provide oxygen for us to breathe, give food and shelter, and can even help combat climate change!

Woodlands cover over 30 percent of Earth's land. They are made up of trees growing closely together, forming a canopy with their branches. Woodlands provide homes for birds, insects, and smaller animals that use the trees for protection against predators.

Trees create oxygen using a clever process called "photosynthesis". They absorb carbon dioxide and energy from the Sun, and breathe out clean oxygen.

O_2

CO_2

Birds build their nests up high among the branches—away from predators looking for a tasty snack!

16

Nature We Eat

Nature can be really tasty! Fruits and vegetables are all parts of a plant. Take a look to see which part of the plant these delicious treats come from.

FLOWERS
The heads of broccoli and cauliflower (the part we eat) are actually the flower buds of their plant.

The clusters on both vegetables are called "florets".

ROOTS
Root vegetables grow underground with one vegetable growing out of each plant.

Carrots, radishes, and parsnips are full of fiber and are super healthy!

FRUIT
Fruits are the fleshy bits of a plant that contain seeds. They can grow low on the ground, like pumpkins, or on trees and bushes.

A pumpkin is a large fruit.

Peas and green beans aren't flowers, but they are the botanical fruit (or seed) of a flowering plant.

Potatoes are called "tubers" because more than one potato comes from one plant.

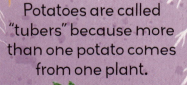

Some vegetables (like peppers and tomatoes) are technically fruit, because they contain seeds!

STEMS

Plant stems can be just as tasty as the flowers and roots.

Because they need to be strong to support their plant, stems are packed with vitamins and minerals.

Celery, asparagus, and rhubarb are all examples of tasty stems.

Be careful with the leaves of a rhubarb plant because these are poisonous!

A garlic bulb is technically a stem!

SEEDS

Seeds are small but mighty—and they can be pretty good to eat too!

Chocolate comes from the cocoa bean, which is a seed that grows on cocoa trees in really hot climates.

Seeds from sunflowers and pumpkins are a perfect snack, filled with goodness.

LEAVES

Tasty leaves include spinach, cabbage, and lettuce. We wouldn't advise munching on tree leaves, though!

We use the leaves of herbs, like rosemary, to flavor our food.

Mushrooms and Other Fungi

There are over 155,000 named fungus species. Fungi feed on other natural organisms while also providing food to the plants and animals around them. Because of this, they are very important for the ecosystem.

Poisonous Toadstools

Although they look pretty, some fungi are poisonous, like the yellow death cap and the red fly agaric. This means they can make us sick.

Spores

Like plants make seeds, mushrooms make spores. They grow just under their caps and blow off in the wind to spread so more mushrooms can grow.

Never eat a mushroom that isn't on your plate!

Lots of mushrooms are safe to eat, like chestnut, portabello, and shitake.

Can you recognize any on this plate?

A fruiting body is the body of the mushroom that grows above ground.

The roots of mushrooms are called hyphae. They can spread above and below the ground and collect nutrients for the mushrooms to eat.

Starfish

This mushroom lives in hot, damp places in the southern hemisphere.

Violet Coral

This purple mushroom looks just like a sea coral, but on land.

Elegant Stinkhorn

This mushroom gets its name from its smell of dung or rotting flesh!

Bleeding Fungus

Red liquid seeps out of the fruit which makes it look like it's bleeding.

Fungi live all over the world and come in many colors! **What colors can you see?**

Some mushrooms are bioluminescent. This means they can glow in the dark! This Jack-O'-Lantern is a lovely orange color by day, but by night, it glows a bright greeny-yellow!

Lichen

Lichens are crusty, leaf-like organisms made up of fungi and algae.

Mold

Mold grows in damp places and makes us sick if we eat it, so steer clear of food speckled with green or black blobs.

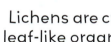

Lichens grow almost anywhere: along walls, rocks, and trees—and even in hot deserts and Arctic tundra.

21

Underground World

The ground under our feet contains millions of organisms. It's also pretty handy for growing food and plants, and it even helps to keep the Earth cool.

The mightiest oak to the smallest daisy all need soil to grow.

Topsoil is where most plants take root and grow. It's the perfect spot for earthworms to make their homes too.

Roots are an important part of any plant. They provide water and nutrients, as well as keeping the plant stable!

Subsoil is made up of sand, silt, and clay with some small rocks mixed in.

22

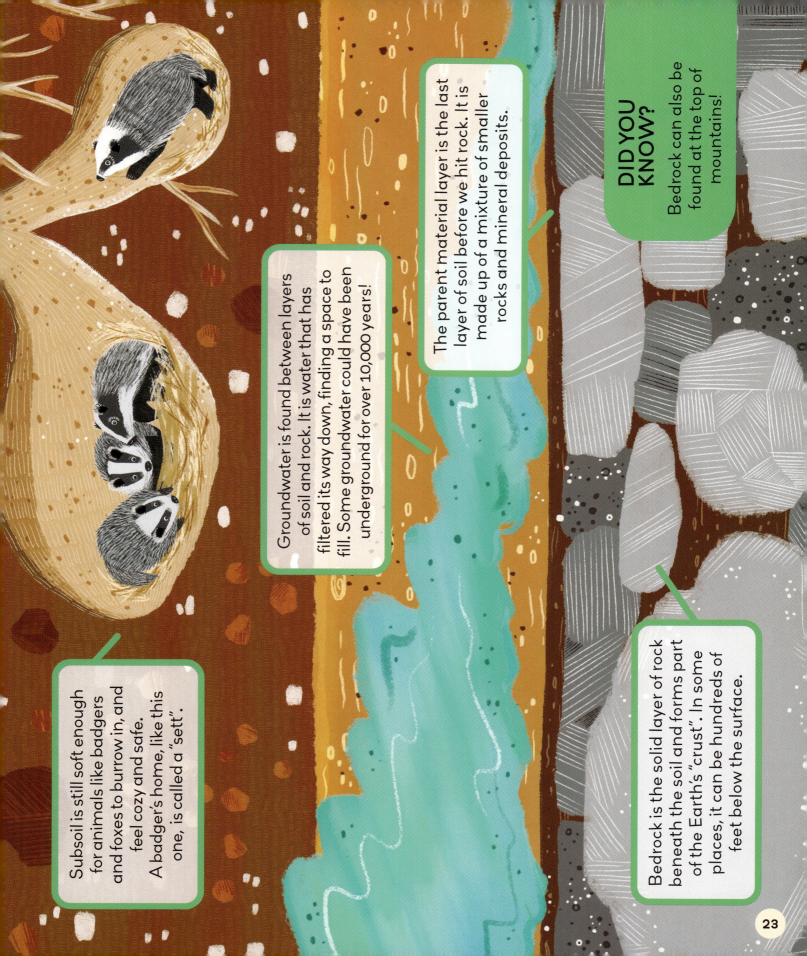

Arctic

The Arctic is at the top of the Earth with the North Pole as the highest point. Both the Arctic and Antarctic are two of the coldest polar regions on Earth, but they are also very different.

The Arctic is an area of frozen ocean that's surrounded by icy land. Antarctica is a continent.

Arctic summer is from June to September, but the Antarctic summer is December to March.

The animals that live in both areas either have thick layers of blubber or fur to keep them warm.

Many animals that live in the Arctic stay all year round and brave the bone-chilling winters.

Who can you spot?

In summer, the Arctic temperature rises above 32°F, which means grass and plants can grow.

DID YOU KNOW?

Only about 10 percent of an iceberg can be seen above sea level!

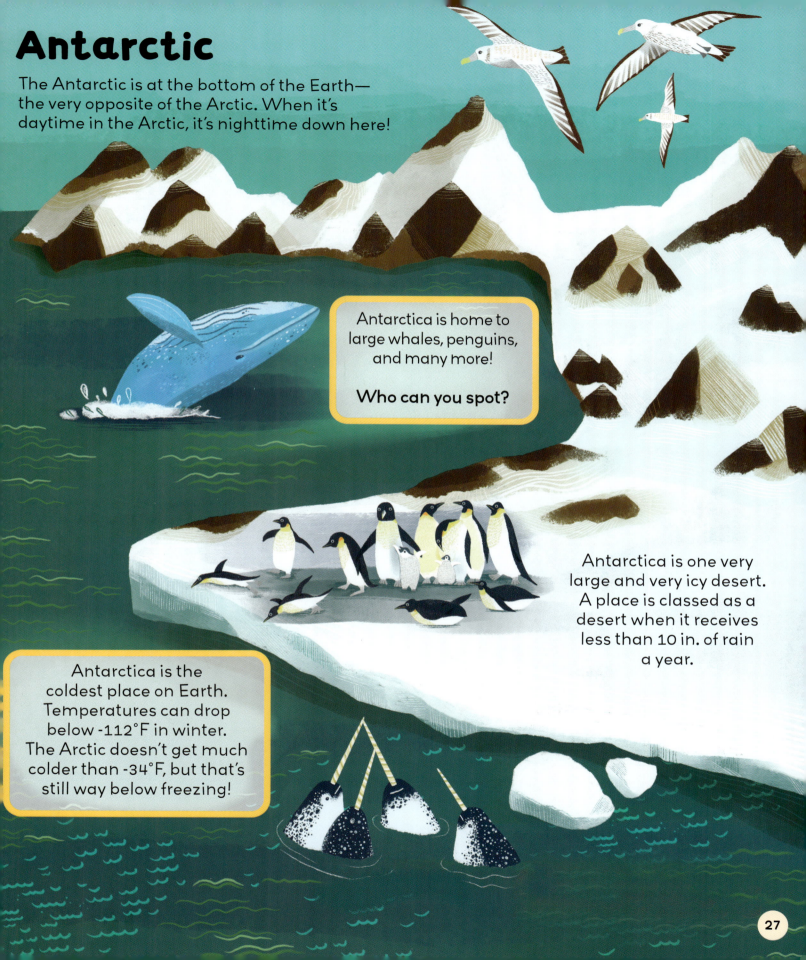

Antarctic

The Antarctic is at the bottom of the Earth—the very opposite of the Arctic. When it's daytime in the Arctic, it's nighttime down here!

Antarctica is home to large whales, penguins, and many more!

Who can you spot?

Antarctica is one very large and very icy desert. A place is classed as a desert when it receives less than 10 in. of rain a year.

Antarctica is the coldest place on Earth. Temperatures can drop below -112°F in winter. The Arctic doesn't get much colder than -34°F, but that's still way below freezing!

Tropical Ocean

Warm, tropical oceans like the Pacific are home to colorful fish and stunning coral reefs. They are very important in helping to keep the Earth's weather in check.

In their warmest spots, tropical oceans can reach 82-86°F. Perfect for the endangered Hawaiian turtle and hammerhead shark!

The Great Barrier Reef is the largest reef system on Earth. It is home to lots of different creatures and is so special it has been put under protection!

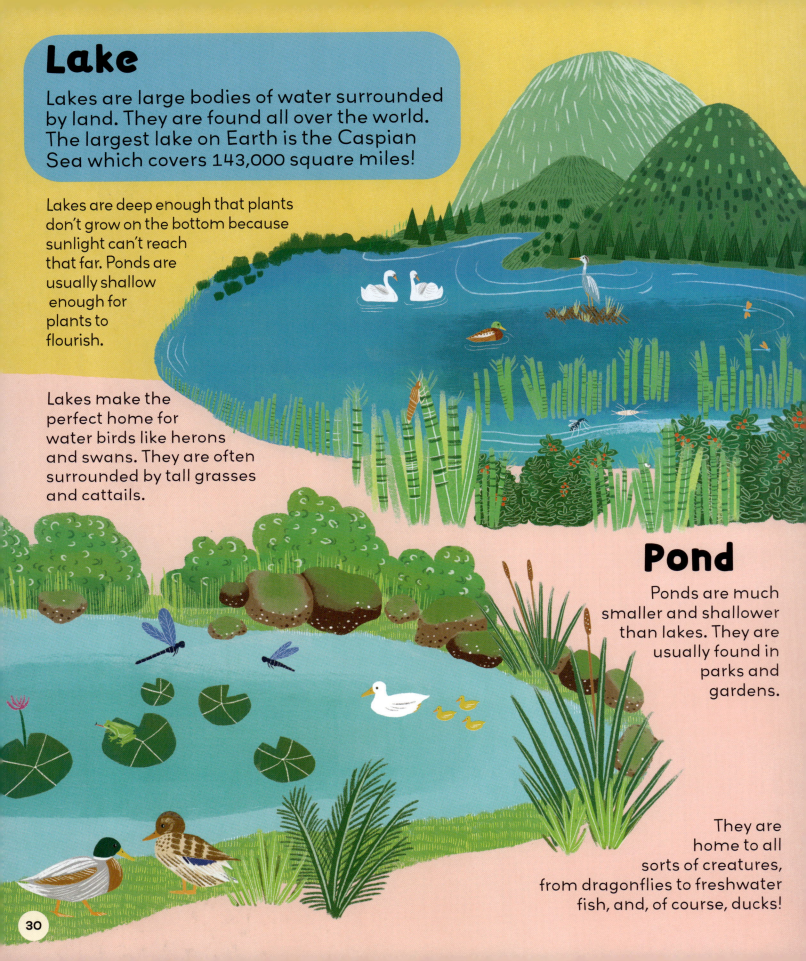

Lake

Lakes are large bodies of water surrounded by land. They are found all over the world. The largest lake on Earth is the Caspian Sea which covers 143,000 square miles!

Lakes are deep enough that plants don't grow on the bottom because sunlight can't reach that far. Ponds are usually shallow enough for plants to flourish.

Lakes make the perfect home for water birds like herons and swans. They are often surrounded by tall grasses and cattails.

Pond

Ponds are much smaller and shallower than lakes. They are usually found in parks and gardens.

They are home to all sorts of creatures, from dragonflies to freshwater fish, and, of course, ducks!

Running Water

Flowing water, such as rivers and waterfalls, are very important. They provide fresh water and food for lots of different animals—including humans!

The longest river on Earth is the Nile. It is over 4,200 miles long and flows through 11 different countries!

Lots of interesting creatures live in rivers. The Amazon river dolphin is the only species of pink dolphin in the world! Rivers are also home to the freshwater turtle, which has been on Earth for about 200 million years.

DID YOU KNOW?

The tallest waterfall in the world is the Angel Falls in Venezuela. It is a huge 3,200 ft tall!

Waterfalls happen when a large body of water flows over the edge of a rock formation (like a cliff). They help to purify water and irrigate the soil around them.

If there is one animal that loves rivers more than any other, it is the beaver. These clever animals make dams out of branches and twigs to create a pond in the river. These ponds protect the beavers from predators.

Mountains and Caves

Mountains are formed over millions of years, when two of the Earth's "plates" bump together. Caves are formed as rainwater gradually wears away the rock.

DID YOU KNOW?

Some mountains are still growing. Mount Everest, in the Himalayas, grows by around 0.16 in. each year.

The four main types of mountain are called: fold, fault-block, dome, and volcanic.

The Barberton Mountains are thought to be over 3 billion years old!

Lichen is a type of organism made up of fungi and algae that grows on rocks. It's the perfect snack for hungry mountain goats.

Crystals are often found in caves due to the high amount of minerals found in them. Cave of the Crystals in Naica, Mexico has some of the largest crystals in the world, that can be as long as 36 ft!

The cones that form on the floor of a cave are called stalagmites.

Stalactites are icicle-shaped stone formations that hang from the ceiling of a cave. They are made by dripping water that leaves a tiny piece of calcium carbonate behind as it falls.

Bats love caves because they are dark and cool. The Bracken Cave in Texas is home to more than 15 million bats!

Ash Clouds
In 79 CE, the eruption of Mount Vesuvius destroyed the Italian town of Pompeii. Everything was covered in stone and ash so quickly that the site is still frozen in time today.

A volcano that has erupted in the last 10,000 years is described as "active". One that could erupt in the future is known as "dormant". A volcano that hasn't erupted in the past 10,000 years is called "extinct".

Ash Layers

Crater
The opening to the volcano where lava spews out.

Branch Pipe
Where lava breaks through the volcano to get to the surface.

Magma Chamber
Where magma is stored.

Bedrock

How are volcanoes formed?
When magma (lava that is found underground) reaches a weak spot in the Earth's crust, it comes out as lava (along with poisonous gases and ash) at temperatures as high as 2,200°F. The lava burns everything in its path before it cools and hardens into a cone shape—making the volcano! The more eruptions a volcano has, the more layers of cooled lava there are and the bigger the volcano becomes.

Even though volcanoes can be dangerous, people still live near them because they produce rich soil that is great for growing crops.

Volcanoes

A volcano is a mountain or hill that allows hot liquid called lava to escape from inside the Earth. They can sometimes cause huge explosions too!

DID YOU KNOW?

The loudest sound ever recorded was from the volcano Krakatoa, in South East Asia. In 1883, it erupted with a boom that was heard nearly 3,100 miles away!

There are thousands of volcanoes on our planet, but not all of them can be seen. Some volcanoes are under the sea or below the ice caps. There are 452 volcanoes in a horseshoe shape in the Pacific Ocean. This is where 75 percent of the world's eruptions happen and it is called the Ring of Fire!

Earthquakes and Tsunamis

The surface of the Earth (or the "crust") is made up of plates that have been moving for millions of years. When these plates touch, it can cause earthquakes and tsunamis.

Crust
The surface we live on.

Mantle
A layer of hot rock that flows like a slow-moving river.

Outer Core
The outer core is made up of liquid iron, nickel and other metals.

Inner Core
A solid ball of iron and nickel that can be as hot as 7,200–9,000°F.

Tectonic Plates
The Earth's crust is split into giant, jigsaw-like pieces called tectonic plates. They move between 3/4 and 4 in. every year!

> Because the Earth's mantle is liquid, it can sometimes make the plates on top of it move. If the plates drag or scrape against each other, the ground will start to shake. The more the plates touch, the bigger the earthquake.

No one knows exactly when an earthquake will happen. Luckily, most are very small. Here's what to do if you're ever inside a building when an earthquake occurs.

Drop
Get on your hands and knees.

Cover

Hide under a table or in a doorway, then cover your head with your arms.

Hold On
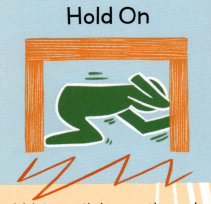
Wait until the earthquake has stopped before you move.

Sometimes an earthquake can occur under the sea. When this happens, the movement in the water above it creates waves. These waves start off quite small, but as they travel toward land, they get bigger and bigger, creating a giant wave called a tsunami.

The strength of an earthquake is measured on the Moment Magnitude Scale. Earthquakes are measured from 1 (the smallest) to 9 (the most powerful).

Scientists who study earthquakes are called seismologists. They record the strength and length of an earthquake using a special device called a seismograph.

The wavy lines that the seismograph draws also help to find out where the earthquake started—its epicenter.

Hurricanes and Tornadoes

Hurricanes and tornadoes are powerful storms with heavy rains and swirling winds. Hurricanes are much larger than tornadoes, but both can be dangerous and destructive.

WEATHER SATELLITE

The Saffir-Simpson Scale measures the strength of a hurricane between 1 and 5. A category 5 hurricane has winds of almost 160 mph and causes the most devastation to homes.

Hurling Hurricanes

LOCATION: Over warm, tropical oceans.

SPEED AND DISTANCE: More than 155 mph and they can travel thousands of miles.

DEVASTATION: In 2005, Hurricane Katrina destroyed over 200,000 homes.

DID YOU KNOW?

Most tornadoes form over land, but when one does happen over water, it is called a "waterspout".

This is the Fujita Scale. It measures intensity of the tornado by the amount of damage it may cause.

73-112 mph

113-157 mph

158-206 mph

207-260 mph

261+ mph

Turbulent Tornadoes

LOCATION: Most tornadoes form in North America.

SPEED AND DISTANCE: Tornadoes can reach wind speeds of 300 mph and travel up to 5 miles.

DEVASTATION: In 2011, 360 tornadoes occurred in the United States, injuring thousands of people.

Meteorologists (scientists who study the weather) measure these powerful winds using a tool called an anemometer or by reading information collected from weather satellites.

41

Weather and Seasons

The weather affects all things. From the clothes we wear, to how we travel, and what food is available to eat. Weather simply means what is happening in the atmosphere, whether it is wet or dry, hot or cold, windy or still.

The stormiest place on Earth is Lake Maracaibo in Venezuela where there are thunderstorms for over 140 days each year!

The windiest place on Earth is Antarctica, where winds can reach over 186 mph.

One of the coldest places on Earth is the East Antarctic Plateau where it can be as chilly as -145°F.

Can you name all of the types of weather on this page?

The rainiest place on Earth is Mawsynram, in India. It gets nearly 470 in. of rain every year.

One of the snowiest places on Earth is the Hakkoda Mountains. They have an average snowfall of 57 ft. per year.

The hottest recorded place on Earth is Furnace Creek in Death Valley, California (USA) which has reached up to 134°F.

When the vapor cools down, clouds form. This is called "condensation".

When the water droplets get heavy, they fall to the ground as rain (or "precipitation").

When the Sun heats this water, it turns (or "evaporates") into vapor.

When this water flows into the rivers, lakes, and sea, it is called "collection."

Water Cycle

What are seasons?

Seasons are caused due to the Earth revolving around the Sun. For one half of the year, the Northern Hemisphere leans toward the Sun; for the other half, the Southern Hemisphere has its turn!

Spring: As the warmer weather returns, plants grow, trees get their leaves back, and animals come out of hibernation.

Summer: This should be the time when the weather is its warmest and there is plenty of food around for wildlife.

Fall: Leaves start to change and fall. Animals prepare for winter by growing thicker coats and lining their homes.

Winter: Some birds fly off to warmer climates, animals hibernate, and some plants close up or die off, ready for new shoots to grow in the spring.

Climate Change

Climate change means the change in temperature of a certain climate caused by global warming. It can have a serious effect on wildlife and the occurrences of extreme weather.

Burning fossil fuels increases global warming. Fossil fuels are fuels that have been formed over millions of years. They release CO2 (carbon dioxide) into the air and are non-renewable, which means that one day, they will run out!

Examples of fossil fuels are natural gas, coal, and the gas and diesel used to power vehicles.

Biomass
Biomass is a renewable energy that can be burned—like wood and natural waste. It gives off far less CO2 than fossil fuels.

Wind Power
Renewable energy is energy made by a source that can be used again and again. Tall wind turbines spin using the power of wind that is then turned into energy

Solar Power
Solar panels capture energy from the Sun, which can be turned into electricity.

Hydropower
Fast-running water can be used to generate electricity and power machines.

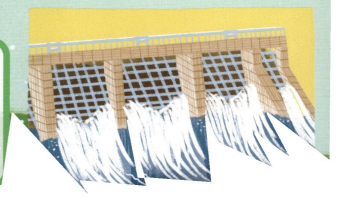

How can I help?

There are lots of ways you can help reduce climate change, just by doing a few small things each day.

Bike or walk short distances instead of using a car!

Reduce

Put leftover food and veggies in the compost bin.

Turn off lights when you leave a room.

Use your own containers and bags when buying food.

Reuse

Search for cool retro clothes in thrift stores.

Donate your old toys and clothes to charity.

Picking up litter from sidewalks and parks is a great way to avoid plastic getting into the ecosystem.

Separate your garbage into the correct recycling bins.

Recycle

Sew up holes and reattach buttons instead of getting new clothes.

Repair

Paint old furniture to "upcycle" it into something new.

When something breaks that you can't fix, see if there is a repair shop nearby to help you.

Index

A
absorption..7
active volcanoes...............................34
adaption..6
algae..12, 21
amphibians.......................................11
Antarctic..............................9, 27, 42
antelopes..24
apex predators........................13, 31
Arctic...21, 26, 29
ash, volcanic...................................36
autumn..43

B
badgers..23
bears..26
beavers..33
bedrock......................................22, 36
bees..14
bioluminescence............................21
biomass..44
biomes...8–9
birds..........................11, 13, 16, 30
bleeding fungi................................21
branch pipes...................................36
breathing..7
burrows..23
bustards..24
butterflies..................................14–15

C
caddisflies..11
carnivores..................................11–12
caves..34
climate change........................43–44
coast redwoods..............................16
coniferous forests............................7
coral reefs.......................................27
core..37

D
cow parsley.....................................15
craters..36
crust..23, 36, 38
crystals...35

D
dams..33
decomposers..................................12
deserts................................9, 25, 27
dormant volcanoes.......................36
dragonflies......................................30
ducks..30

E
Earth...38
earthquakes............................38–39
earthworms....................................22
elegant stinkhorn..........................21
epicentres.......................................39
excretion..7

F
fish...11, 12–13
flowering plants......10, 14–15, 18
food chains............................12–13, 31
forests..8–9, 17
fossil fuels.......................................44
fruiting bodies...............................20
fruits...18
Fujita Scale.....................................41
fungi..12, 20–21

G
giraffes...24
grasses...12
grasshoppers.................................12
grasslands..................................8, 24
groundwater..................................23
growth..7

H
habitats..................................8–9, 13
hares..26
hawks...13
hemispheres..................................43
herbivores.......................................12
honeysuckle...................................15
hoverflies..15
hurricanes................................40–41
hydropower....................................44
hydrothermal vents.....................29
hyphae...20

I
inner core..38
insects..11, 14
invertebrates...........................10–11

K
kingfishers......................................13
krill..12

L
lakes...30
lava...31
leaves...32
lichen..21, 34
life...6–7
lions..13, 24
liverworts..10

M
magma...36
mammals..10
mantle..38
marsupials......................................10
meteorologists..............................41
microbes..11
microscopic life.............................11

46